OUT OF THE SHADOWS

Roger Lane

HALSGROVE

First published in Great Britain in 2009

British Library Cataloguing-in-Publication Data
A CIP record for this title is available from the British Library

ISBN 978 1 84114 925 7

HALSGROVE
Halsgrove House,
Ryelands Industrial Estate,
Bagley Road, Wellington, Somerset TA21 9PZ
Tel: 01823 653777   Fax: 01823 216796
email: sales@halsgrove.com

Part of the Halsgrove group of companies.
Information on all Halsgrove titles is available at: www.halsgrove.com

Printed and bound by Grafiche Flaminia, Italy

"*Inevitably we leave Monte Carlo thinking that this Motor Racing lark is fine, God's in his heaven, wines in the bottle, pictures in the can and all's well with the world…*"

"*To photograph racing cars racing, and to have them look as if they are racing, you must get in close, really close – much too close in fact for comfort. When you get up from crouching beside the track with exhaust marks across your face you're getting near it…*"

Motoring writer Michael Frostick on working with motor racing photographer – Louis Klemantaski – 1960 (Michael Frostick was the main caption writer for the photographs of Louis Klemantaski)

We gratefully acknowledge Batsford, an imprint of Anova Books Company Ltd for the right to use quotations by Michael Frostick from 'A Day at the Races' published in *The Motorist's Weekend Book* edited by Michael Frostick and Anthony Harding and published by B.T.Batsford Ltd in 1960.

Acknowledgements

During the late 1960s when I was photographing the motor racing scene I had no idea that one day my photographs would result in a book. I would therefore like to thank all those who have along the way and over the years provided me with the opportunity and encouragement to see these images 'come out of the shadows'...

Roger Holman for introducing me to Avon Tyrell – where the story began
John Shire and Audrey Tapson of Agfa Gevaert's Advertising Dept (1968)
Gordon Cruickshank – Deputy Editor of *Motor Sport*
Richard Copeman – www.historicracing.com
Kay Browning for the loan of her image of Lorenzo Bandini at Monaco GP 1967
Brian House for his continued encouragement and critique

Introduction

I am sure every amateur photographer aspires to experience life on the professional side of the camera at some time in their life, but not all achieve that opportunity. Although still an 'amateur' photographer after more than forty years behind the lens, I consider myself extremely fortunate in having been given many photographic experiences over the years.

Perhaps I have just been lucky or in the right place at the right time but I must admit to always having a photographic project in hand which tends to provide a concentrated focus and may have been instrumental in some opportunities coming my way.

Photography for me started in the 1960s and to some extent complemented my interest in motor racing. As a member of a local car club I frequently carried out photography at meetings.

Having become an official with the British Automobile Racing Club, races offered the chance to wander around the paddock during lunch breaks. I photographed the cars and drivers with my Werra and fixed Tessar lens, later progressing to a Praktica SLR with a Tessar 50mm lens, 30mm Lydith wide angle, 135mm and 180mm manual preset telephotos. The latter were used for action shots taken from spectator enclosures when not on duty.

Motor racing and photography also combined well during a visit to the Monaco Grand Prix in 1967. On my return I decided to make more of photography and joined my local camera club. In many ways this was a turning point.

Wimborne Camera Club was a very forward thinking and active organisation. At the time I joined they were about to start on a new venture of photographic seminars held at Avon Tyrell, an old country house in the New Forest.

It was at one of these events that I met John Shire, then Advertising Manager for Agfa Gevaert. John was very keen to promote their new Agfa CT18 colour film. After seeing some of my motor racing images it was suggested I photograph the international motor racing scene for the Agfa Gevaert lecture programme.

I was given a brief of capturing the sport's atmosphere and colour; not just the action shots but the drivers, teams and personalities, mechanics and cars. Audrey Tapson, John Shire's personal assistant arranged the necessary 'Photographer' passes and fifty rolls of Agfa CT18 arrived on my doorstep; the rest was up to me.

It helped of course that I knew my way around the circuits as a motor racing official. Motor racing is a dangerous sport and one must always be aware of this fact, not just out on the circuit but also in the pits and paddock where cars are being manoeuvred. Equally important one should know when to photograph drivers at close quarters. In reality I always found the drivers and teams of that era very approachable and helpful.

I was also rather conscious of my 'amateur' status, particularly with a Praktica around my neck when mixing it with the professional sports photographers and their Nikon Fs. However undaunted, I continued to concentrate on capturing the images within my set brief.

I had many amusing experiences but towards the end of my assignment with Agfa, extreme hilarity was caused when I signed on in the press office one morning for an event at Thruxton as representing Agfa Gevaert. What was so amusing about that? This major event was being sponsored by Kodak!

It was altogether a unique experience to photograph my favourite sport and one which provided me with a greater appreciation of photography. I had always admired the work of Louis Klemantaski and his book *For Practice Only* and Horst Baumann's photography in Ken Purdy's book *The New Matadors*. I wouldn't like to say that I have achieved anything close to their classic images but I would like to think that in some small way they may have influenced me when composing in the viewfinder.

The late sixties was an era of motor racing which was very experimental and at times tragic but it did have a rather family atmosphere surrounding it. Seemingly teams helped each other out and the drivers, although competitive on the track, always had a respect for their counterparts and the rules of the sport. Friendship and support always showed through particularly during moments of tragedy and as the seasons progressed safety became a significant priority. It was an era which I feel very honoured to have witnessed and recorded. It was not long before the motor racing scene changed considerably, becoming far more commercial and increasingly regulated but most importantly a much safer sport.

When the images were received back from Agfa I set about putting together 'Race', an audio visual feature using dissolve projection, commentary and soundtrack. Since then the images have been stored until I retired. I have since scanned and revived some of the faded images in Photoshop and placed them on my website, where they have received significant interest from magazines and authors researching or writing about motor racing in the '60s.

I may never have made it as a full time professional photographer but I certainly had a tremendous experience. In today's very commercial and highly regulated Formula 1 scene I doubt such an opportunity for an amateur photographer could ever be repeated.

Looking back on this experience some forty years later, I regard the images I captured at Monaco in 1967 as those which most impressed Agfa Gevaert's John Shire and so presented me with such an opportunity. It is therefore most appropriate that the photographs taken in Monaco's shadowy late afternoon light should also have inspired the title for this book, in fact having been stored away for so long perhaps all my motor racing photographs are now Out of the Shadows.

Roger Lane July 2009

Opposite:
Graham Hill at Silverstone, March 1969.

British Grand Prix Silverstone 1963

I make no apologies for including this view of Silverstone as the opening shot in my book of motor racing photographs.

This image was I think my very first 'real' motor racing photograph and was certainly my first view of the circuit as I crossed the famous footbridge from the car park behind the grandstands to the much respected inner sanctum of the paddock and pits area.

Practice for the support races for the 16th British Grand Prix was in progress and even now I can feel the chill down my spine and a tingling sensation of excitement. The sight and sound of a red GT Ferrari came hurtling towards me, Jack Sears at the wheel, braking and changing down, emitting that wonderful sound that only a Ferrari can produce. It made its way at astonishing speed into Copse and accelerated away towards Maggots.

I was just eighteen and despite having had an interest in both aviation and motor racing from my early school days I had spent many hours at the local airport (Hurn) now Bournemouth International but in motor racing terms had only previously experienced local club events, autocross, sprints and hill climbs. This was my very first visit to a motor race circuit and my introduction was the British Grand Prix. Little did I know at that stage how my involvement with the sport was to pan out and how very close I was to come to the action.

I am writing this almost 45 years to the day later, in the knowledge that the spectacle of a British Grand Prix at Silverstone has only one more year to run before Donnington takes on the challenge of hosting Britain's premier race.

Progress has to be made in any sport or business but Silverstone has always been regarded as the home of British motor racing and for me that will never change. It was the very first circuit I saw a Formula 1 car perform and where the magical names I had only read about suddenly became a reality.

I now have wonderful memories of my marshalling days at Silverstone and even more as a photographer. We may have lost the British Grand Prix at Silverstone but the memories will linger on and I have been fortunate enough to have witnessed and captured just some of Silverstone's historic and treasured moments.

My first view of Silverstone.

The Silverstone Paddock

My first visit to Silverstone was on the Friday practice day, not only were tickets cheaper but there was the possibility of entering the paddock with a pass for just £1 and seeing the cars being prepared up close.

At this stage in my 'photographic career' I only possessed a 35mm East German Werra camera with a fixed Tessar lens of 50mm. This meant track photography was somewhat distant but the camera was ideal for capturing the scenes behind the pits where the cars could be photographed being prepared and worked on prior to practice sessions.

The Silverstone paddock in those days was a very friendly sort of place but in many ways so was the sport. The gravel imbedded stones in the cars' grooved tyres but was the only surface available for the mechanics. Picket fences kept people out of official areas and drivers and entrants sat around on picnic chairs beside their converted coaches or ex removal vans which transported the cars. Everyone appeared to know everyone else and it seemed almost a family atmosphere.

Drivers seemed to have time to chat to spectators and were often seen and heard having conversations with one another over the lines through Maggots or Stowe and what gears were preferable for the circuit. When I say one another I don't mean team mates, I mean conversations between competitors. Imagine that happening now in the fiercely competitive sport we have today where strategy in the pits plays as big a part as the driving.

Cockpit of John Surtees' F1 Ferrari
– Silverstone July 1963.

Swedish driver Jo Bonnier's Cooper Climax is prepared in the Silverstone paddock. This car was entered by privateer Rob Walker who for many seasons provided the cars for Stirling Moss's eminent career.

Practice Day and the View from the Pits

Having only a standard 50mm lens on a 35mm camera, my trackside photography was limited but the Silverstone pits provided the answer. Here you could lean over the rails above the small pits enclosures, still with the aid of a £1 paddock pass and capture the action either on the track as the cars exited Woodcote corner or as they entered the pits for adjustment immediately below.

I well remember almost missing my shot of Jim Clark entering the pits. At the time the 27 year old Scottish farmer had narrowly missed winning the 1962 world championship to Graham Hill and was determined not to let the 1963 championship slip from his grasp. During practice he was really setting the pace and it seemed he was never going to come in, when eventually he dived into the pits I was in the process of drinking a cup of coffee and just managed to grab this shot one handed. Incidentally Jim Clark went on to win the 1963 British Grand Prix (his fourth grand prix victory in a row) from the Ferrari of John Surtees and Graham Hill's BRM which spluttered over the line in third place with empty fuel tanks.

My other shots from that position above the pits were of American Richie Ginther, team mate to Graham Hill with the work's BRM and one of motor racing's more colourful characters, Innes Ireland driving the privately entered British Racing Partnership BRM 'T' car (test or practice car).

Richie Ginther eventually followed his team mate Graham Hill into fourth position in the race but Innes Ireland was plagued with ignition problems and failed to finish despite achieving tenth position on the grid.

Opposite: Jim Clark enters the pits in his Lotus Climax - Silverstone 1963.

Innes Ireland in the British Racing Partnership BRM passes the Woodcote Corner Grandstands – Silverstone July 1963.

Richie Ginther in the Owen Racing Partnership BRM exits Woodcote Corner – Silverstone 1963.

The Donald Healey Cars entry for Christabel Carlisle was this 1098cc Austin Healey Sprite GT photographed from the bridge as the car headed for Copse. Silverstone July 1963.

Supporting Races

Every British Grand Prix has been supported by other races and in July 1963 the event was supported with an International 'Formula Junior' event for single seater racing cars with 1098cc engines. Formula Junior was the stepping stone for Grand Prix status and such names as Denny Hulme, Pete Revson, Richard Attwood, Pete Arundell and Mike Spence appeared in this race. Denny Hulme went on to become World Champion in 1967.

A Production Touring Car Race and a GT and Sports Car Race also supported the event and provided me with photo opportunities in the Silverstone paddock. I could not resist capturing the cars in the paddock, particularly the ultimate Ferrari GT car for Jack Sears. These Ferraris now reach incredible values at auction but in 1963 winning such an event would only have earned prize money of £40 with £20 for second place and £10 for third.

The Formula Junior Event however would have earned the winner the BRDC trophy and £100.

Winning the Formula 1 British Grand Prix however produced winnings of £750 for first place, £350 for second and £125 for third, reducing to £20 for eighth place.

The Maranello Concessionaires Ferrari GT for Jack Sears entered in the International GT and Sports Car Race – Silverstone July 1963.

Glorious Goodwood Days

The International Trophy meeting at Goodwood on Easter Monday always heralded the start of the motor racing season. As I recall it was invariably cold and showery if not downright wet. However, it always produced exciting racing in a beautiful setting beneath the Sussex Downs.

It was the meeting not to miss as it produced new drivers, cars and teams either in Formula 2 or Formula 1 races. As a member of the British Automobile Racing Club (BARC), I started my marshalling duties at Goodwood so was not always available to photograph the racing action. On one occasion, I can't remember why I was not marshalling but I went as a spectator and wielded my new (but secondhand) 35mm Praktica SLR camera with 135mm telephoto lens.

Goodwood had a number of excellent viewing locations but the members' enclosure on the inside of the track provided a wonderful view of the famous Goodwood chicane. This was an area where many races were lost and won and enabled me to capture shots of the cars and drivers against a splendid backdrop of a crowd-filled grandstand. These images remind me so much of the wonderful days spent at Goodwood and the atmosphere the circuit provided.

Like Silverstone, Goodwood as a motor racing circuit was a by-product of the Second World War. As a left-over aerodrome with a perimeter track it was ideal as a motor racing circuit. Bomber Command provided Silverstone and Fighter Command provided Goodwood or West Hampnett as it was then called. Apparently it was Australian racing driver Tony Gaze who used to land his Hurricane at West Hampnett as an RAF pilot who came up with the idea, and so it was that Goodwood became a motor racing circuit, situated on rolling farmland owned by the Duke of Richmond and Gordon.

It was 1966 when the final race took place at Goodwood when the circuit was forced to close on public safety grounds. The BARC however found a new home circuit at Thruxton in Hampshire but today the true spirit of motor racing survives at Goodwood thanks to Lord March who has pioneered the International Festival of Speed and the unique and atmospheric Goodwood Revival meetings.

Graham Hill (BRM) exits the Goodwood chicane in front of an Easter Monday crowd.

Jack Brabham in his characteristic cockpit style exits the chicane on a drying track.

Monaco Grand Prix 1967

I travelled down to Monaco with friends for my first experience of a European Grand Prix. It is interesting to note that in those days any spending money taken out of the country was recorded in your passport and mine records that I took just £25 with me.

The race was marred by an horrific accident to Ferrari driver Lorenzo Bandini but was won by New Zealander Denny Hulme in a Brabham. It was his first grand prix win and he went on to become the 1967 World Champion.

We had scoured the course for the best vantage point and eventually decided on the steps leading down from the Casino Gardens and took up our positions early on Saturday for the practice sessions and supporting races; it rained as I recall.

The steps and balustrade provided a view of the cars as they exited the Mirabeau Corner in front of the hotel of that name and down the hill to what was then named the Station Hairpin. This slightly elevated position provided the ability to look down on the cars as they cut in close to the balustrade while setting up and braking for the hairpin. Cockpit designs in those days meant the spectator was able to view the gear changing and preferred driving styles of the maestros as they went about their balance of routines lap after lap. It was this position that enabled me to take one of my favourite images of Graham Hill at the wheel of the Lotus BRM.

During practice Graham broke second gear on his Hewland gearbox only to find there was no spare available in the Lotus team. Eventually Colin Chapman managed to borrow a spare from Bob Anderson the privateer who was running the same gearbox. Second gear at Monaco is extremely important as the course twists its way around the streets of the principality with its many turns and gradients. It was a valiant effort for Graham to put the fragile Lotus on the fourth row of the grid. During the race however Graham kept a consistent rhythm going despite a slipping clutch, damaged chassis and a broken suspension, eventually nursing the car home in second place behind Denny Hulme in the Brabham.

Denny Hulme exits the Station Hairpin on his way to winning the 25th Monaco GP in his 3 litre Repco Brabham.

Action at the wheel for Bruce McLaren in his McLaren BRM V8 as he rounds the Station Hairpin in fourth place.

Graham Hill Lotus 33 with 2 litre BRM Engine.

Monaco Light

Opposite:

Jackie Stewart passes the Hotel Mirabeau in his BRM V8 Monaco 1967.

It has been said many times that visiting a Monaco Grand Prix is an experience not to be missed. Of all the grands prix, Monaco's situation on the Mediterranean coast overlooked by the royal palace with the harbour, hotels, casino and gardens lining the course makes it a very colourful and glamorous place to be. Add the sight and sound of the grand prix cars making their way around the narrow streets with no margin for error and you have the recipe for a grand prix with atmosphere. Monaco also has a colourful racing history: what other grand prix circuit can claim cars disappearing into a harbour for example? But for me as an aspiring photographer at my favourite sport, Monaco's light had a tremendous appeal.

Saturday practice was just a little damp but during the late afternoon I noticed the shadows across the track and decided to shoot the cars as they came through the shadows outside the Hotel Mirabeau and down to the hairpin. This was Mediterranean light at its best – all I had to do was get the exposure right. Thanks to my trusty Weston exposure meter and light readings taken direct from the track surface I captured some atmospheric racing images.

My favourite is Jackie Stewart's BRM passing the Hotel Mirabeau through the afternoon shadows. I have this print hanging in the lounge at home as a constant reminder of that atmospheric moment.

Unfortunately during the race Jackie Stewart retired with a damaged crown wheel but Chris Amon finished in third place behind Graham Hill's Lotus despite having to pit with a punctured rear tyre.

Chris Amon's Ferrari on its way to the Station Hairpin Monaco 1967.

Lorenzo Bandini rounds the Station Hairpin in his Ferrari.
Shortly after this picture was taken he crashed heavily on the harbour side, an accident from which he never recovered.

Lorenzo Bandini

The 1967 Monaco Grand Prix was marred by the tragic accident of Ferrari's driver Lorenzo Bandini.

The previous year Bandini had set the Monaco lap record but during the Friday morning practice when exiting the Mirabeau Corner the car appeared to veer across the circuit, making contact with the wall beneath the Casino Gardens and damaging the front suspension.

The Ferrari mechanics had straightened out the Ferrari in time for the next F1 practice late on Saturday afternoon. Seemingly unaffected by Friday's incident Bandini was in hot pursuit of pole position going faster than ever. However Jack Brabham had been stretching the legs of his new Repco engine and put in his final practice lap to take pole position from Lorenzo Bandini who was relegated to the inside front row of the grid.

During the race it was Bandini who led the field through St Devote; however Jack Brabham's new Repco engine broke a connecting rod and was throwing oil on to his rear tyres. Brabham spun at Mirabeau, facing a charging herd of cars who managed to get round him, leaving a surprised Brabham reversing down the hill to the Station Hairpin.

After much re-positioning, Bandini found himself behind Denny Hulme who was revelling in the performance of the Brabham. Bandini was determined not to let him go and quickened his pace but on lap 82 as he took the chicane on the harbour front, the Ferrari struck the wooden barriers and careered into straw bales landing back on the track upside down. Almost instantaneously the car was engulfed in flames and despite brave efforts by the marshals, Bandini subsequently died from his burns.

Taken during the Friday morning practice session when Bandini lost control exiting the Mirabeau and collided with the wall damaging the front suspension. Photo courtesy Kay Browning (who took this image with nothing more than an Instamatic camera).

Martini International 300 Trophy Race – Silverstone 1968

The Lure of Sports Car Racing

The thrilling sight and sound of sports car racing is always a major attraction and the Martini Trophy at Silverstone is no exception. This was one event in the year which attracted an international entry and provided spectators with the opportunity of seeing prototype sports cars and GT cars competing at high speed. These cars, many of which also competed in the Le Mans Twenty Four Hour race were extremely powerful and very fast, providing a colourful, noisy and thrilling spectacle. The aerodynamic shape of the sports cars and their highly tuned and developed engines meant they were often faster in a straight line than Formula 1 cars.

Opposite: "One day I want to be a racing driver". Australian Frank Gardner's 3 litre prototype Ford sports (P3L) car in the red and gold colours of Alan Mann Racing provides a dream for a young spectator in the Silverstone paddock. During the race this car on its first outing at Silverstone established the lead straight from the grid and had a memorable lap swapping race with New Zealander Denny Hulme in a Lola T70 until retiring with with a broken oil pipe. During their outstanding race both the Lola and the prototype Ford were lapping at average speeds approaching 120mph.

Jackie Ickx in the Ferrari keeps the McLarens at bay as he enters Druids.

The British Grand Prix – Brands Hatch July 1968

A Day of Breakdowns

I seldom photographed at Brands Hatch but in July 1968 I decided it was time to witness another grand prix and so headed off towards Kent for a day at the races.

Brands Hatch offers the spectator an amazing natural grandstand as the cars leave the start and finish line before plunging down Paddock Hill Bend and up the hill into Druids. The plunge down is a real heart stopper but there is little time for the driver to blink before he is positioning the car for the tight right-hander at Druids.

Druids for the spectator meant an uninterrupted view of the cars negotiating Paddock Hill Bend and racing up to the hill. This is where I watched much of the race on that Saturday afternoon.

It was certainly a race of events with sudden rain causing much indecision among the teams just before the start. Those electing to stay with dry tyres made the right decisions when the rain came to nothing. Reliability was the big issue though, as only nine cars of the twenty which left the grid managed to make the finish.

This event was not only proving troublesome for the cars but also for me as half way through the grand prix my camera refused to wind on after each exposure and finally locked up on me completely. This prevented me from photographing the popular Swiss driver Jo Siffert winning the grand prix for the private entrant Rob Walker in his new Lotus 49B.

However it was an interesting race and allowed me to photograph Jochen Rindt in the Brabham Repco V8 who eventually retired on lap 56, needing a small fire to be extinguished and the Belgian driver Jackie Ickx with the wonderful-sounding Ferrari V12 who brought the car home in third place behind team mate New Zealander, Chris Amon.

Brands Hatch, July 1968. Jochen Rindt in Formula 1 Brabham Repco.

The Race of Champions, Brands Hatch 1969

My First Agfa Assignment

It was a bitterly cold, wet and foggy drive from Dorset to Brands Hatch in March 1969 but I was fired up with enthusiasm and fully intended to get my first pictures as a 'commissioned' photographer for Agfa Gevaert.

My brief was to photograph the international motor racing scene, capturing the colour and atmosphere on and off the track to promote Agfa's CT18 colour film. This was my first assignment and I had visions of brilliant red Ferraris, green and yellow Brabhams, orange McLarens and French blue Matras all posing for my camera surrounded by the well-heeled international jet set in the paddock.

Well I had the right idea but this was England in March and the weather left a lot to be desired. There was no sun and on the morning of practice the trees at Druids Hill bend could hardly be seen through the fog.

There was also more news – an announcement from Race Control confirmed there would be no red Ferraris present at this meeting. Chris Amon's car was not ready and with this race not earning any championship points the car was withdrawn.

However I did wander around the paddock area collecting some images. Mechanics working on a BRM outside the Brands Hatch garages, just like a lock up at home really!!! Jack Brabham didn't look particularly happy either sitting in the cockpit of his car now fitted with a new Cosworth engine, replacing the previous Repco power units. He later seemed much more delighted on his return to the paddock after his very promising practice runs.

The cars were now sprouting wings designed to introduce downforce and therefore improve roadholding and traction. This was the start of the pioneering days of aerodynamics in motor racing. Aesthetically it took some getting used to and being a bit of a purist where racing cars are concerned I have to admit to not being very enthusiastic about them. They were certainly not photogenic and here was I on my first assignment – not a good start.

Opposite:
Mechanics prepare the Reg Parnell-entered BRM V12 for Mexican driver Pedro Rodriguez. Note the facilities at Brands Hatch in 1969 compared with the clean, spacious laboratory conditions mechanics work in at today's grand prix circuits .

Jack Brabham takes things seriously as he gets ready for practice powered by his new Cosworth engine.

Behind the Scenes

Compared with the clinical excellence of today's grand prix scene, the famous 'lock ups' at Brands Hatch are a world away. However, when I photographed these scenes from the edge of the paddock looking down on what activity there was on this cold, rather damp morning I could not envisage the luxury and change which the grand prix scene would soon be going through. Advertising and major sponsorship deals were about to change the face of motor racing.

Today Formula 1 is big business and the small man with his own team has very little chance of success or for that matter even getting an entry. But here we see two entries from former fifties racing driver Reg Parnell and Surrey timber merchant Ken Tyrell with their own teams fighting it out with the likes of Ferrari, McLaren, Lotus, BRM and Brabham.

The atmosphere around the drivers was also much more relaxed than we see today. The F1 scene was like a big family, everyone knew everyone and socialised off the track irrespective of who their team was. On the track there was of course always the will to win and a competitive spirit, but with an element of respect.

The Race of Champions was always the British season opener and as such was usually treated by the teams as a testing ground for their new cars or modifications. Although much testing would have been done throughout the winter months, usually in the warmer climates of Europe, this was the first opportunity to test cars in race conditions.

At this early stage in the year Ken Tyrell could never have envisaged what lay ahead for him, his team and his driver Jackie Stewart for the 1969 season.

Ken Tyrell inspects his team's new Matra Ford MS80 for Jackie Stewart while the Reg Parnell mechanics work on the Pedro Rodriguez BRM in the Brands Hatch garages.

Opposite:
"So what's this new Matra like Jackie?" Jackie Stewart (Matra Ford) and Pedro Rodriguez (Reg Parnell BRM) in conversation before the start of practice for The Race of Champions.

Jackie Stewart Prepares for Practice

From my advantaged position looking over the paddock fence I had a good view of the garages below and spotted Jackie Stewart getting ready for the practice session. As I took several pictures, he was seen having a chat with Pedro Rodriguez whose team were in the next garage, getting into his fire proof overalls while having a friendly banter with a mechanic and eventually being hurried away by team boss Ken Tyrell. I felt a bit like a paparazzi photographer but looking back on it now these images present a striking contrast with today's Formula 1 scene.

It was the season opener and the new Matra MS80 was as yet unraced. Ken Tyrell had also brought along the previous year's MS10 with which Jackie Stewart had won the 1968 South African Grand Prix; but it was the new MS80 which Jackie put on the front row of the grid alongside Graham Hill's Lotus 49 for this race.

Come the day of the race, immediately the flag fell Jackie Stewart was in the lead and that afternoon the Brands Hatch spectators witnessed a classic drive where man and machine really came together. The new Ken Tyrell Matra MS80 with Stewart at the wheel outclassed everybody for the entire 50 laps. It was without question a demonstration of superiority and a precursor for the world championship year.

Graham Hill was a creditable second with Denny Hulme in the McLaren third but it was Jackie Stewart and the MS80 who received the standing ovation.

Being hurried away for the practice session by team boss Ken Tyrell.

32

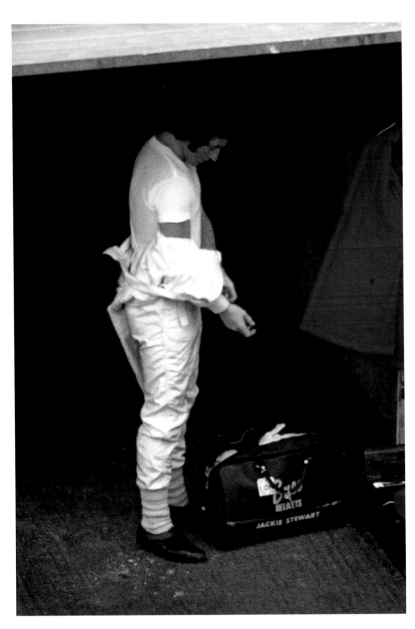

Jackie Stewart prepares for a practice session in the garages at Brands Hatch Race of Champions 1969.

A friendly word for a mechanic before the start of practice.

21st International *Daily Express* Trophy – Silverstone March 1969

Cars Exposed

Motor racing is a very technical sport and this was another side which had to be portrayed. Stripped down cars, mechanics at work and the tools of their trade all made an image which said something about the sport.

Photographing the cars at very close quarters while stripped for preparation or repair was something I was always conscious of. Would someone think I was from the opposition, stealing vital technical secrets? So I always asked first, just in case but I never received a "no": in fact I often had explanations given to me about what was happening. In hindsight I think I was frequently taken for a racing journalist as occasionally my arm band and pass would say 'Press' rather than 'Photographer'.

Concentration – making ready for practice.
This shot was taken on a cold damp morning at Silverstone, no spacious, clean, undercover working conditions here.

Matra cockpit exposed.

McLaren F1.

Setting the Scene

Part of my brief with Agfa was to capture the atmosphere and activity in and around the paddock. As soon as I had arrived at the circuit I wandered around with a medium telephoto lens. This was the best way of isolating certain features of interest. I focused on the ticket and programme sellers, spectators, pit crew preparations and the general scene and buzz of activity going on around me. There was always an air of expectancy as spectators rushed to take up their positions around the track or in grandstand seats. Drivers and teams prepared themselves for practice sessions and the marshals drove out to their posts around the circuit.

Programme seller in the Silverstone paddock. Money exposed on the table and programmes ready to be blown about by the wind.

Pit crew member with driver's helmet and stop watch at the ready.

Inside the Silverstone Pits

Beneath the Silverstone pits viewing area there were a series of 'bunkers' or pit garages providing access to the pit area for mechanics and their equipment.

These also provided the perfect spot for me to take some unusual behind the scenes images.

Once again, always during practice periods, I would wander from one to the other peeping through the rear entrance from the paddock to see what was going on and just occasionally a picture would present itself.

Amongst all the racing paraphernalia of spare tyres, tools, jacks, cylinders, oil and grease the aperture looking out into the pit area would provide an image framed that I just had to have. Silverstone was the only circuit where this seemed to happen.

Today the new pit areas would not provide such a facility for a photographer and these remain some of my favourite images from that time.

Inside the Lotus pit where Graham Hill's distinctive helmet in the colours of the London Rowing Club rests on the front of the car during practice.

View from inside McLaren's Silverstone pit with the fire proof overralled legs of Denny Hulme (left) and Bruce McLaren (right).

Behind the Scenes with Gold Leaf Team Lotus – A Story Unfolds

From my favourite position inside the Silverstone pit area, sometimes an interesting set of pictures would emerge, telling something of the behind the scenes activities.

On one such occasion I was able to capture a few moments while Graham Hill prepared for an attempt to achieve pole position.

From inside the Lotus pit I was able to look up and photograph him readying himself for the off and finally receiving his instructions from Lotus chief Colin Chapman.

Graham Hill fits his fire proof face mask…

…dons his helmet…

…and receives final instructions from team boss Colin Chapman.

Graham Hill

Graham Hill was teamed with the Austrian driver Jochen Rindt with the Gold Leaf Team Lotus 49B cars powered by Cosworth V8 engines. The practice session on Saturday morning was wet and Graham Hill seemed to be having trouble setting the car up.

During the race he had a considerable duel with Pedro Rodriguez in the Parnell BRM and managed to finish in seventh place ahead of the Mexican but only after being lapped by his team mate Jochen Rindt who seemed to positively revel in the wet conditions.

Graham Hill discusses the car's performance during morning practice.

Graham Hill waits patiently. It was interesting to watch the mannerisms of the drivers as they waited in their cars for adjustments to suspension, tyres or wings.

Jochen Rindt and a Classic Drive

For the *Daily Express* Trophy Jochen Rindt had joined Gold Leaf Team Lotus alongside Graham Hill driving the V8 Cosworth Lotus 49Bs and seemed to settle in with the car even in the damp conditions of the day.

During the race I well remember his stunning drive. Initially the car spluttered its way round in wet conditions but after lap six the engine appeared to 'dry out' allowing Jochen to storm through the field in pursuit of Jack Brabham who had led away from the start.

At one stage during his drive through the field, Rindt came up behind his team-mate Graham Hill battling with Pedro Rodriguez and Jackie Ickx racing Piers Courage.

In almost one overtaking move Jochen Rindt passed all four cars and continued in pursuit of Jack Brabham in first place, finishing just 2.2 seconds behind the winning Australian.

It was an historic drive from Jochen Rindt and one which will long be remembered from those classic Silverstone days.

Jochen Rindt contemplates the car set up during the Saturday practice session. The weather conditions on that day were not ideal and presented all the teams with a significant challenge.

Pit boards tell the story during the practice session.

Jochen Rindt in the Cosworth V8-powered Lotus 49B enters Woodcote Corner at speed during practice for his memorable drive in the Daily Express Trophy.

Jackie Stewart in discussion with an official during the wet Saturday morning practice session in the Silverstone pits.

Jackie Stewart Portraits

Driver portraits were high on the list of Agfa priorities, so I had to get in close, sometimes with just a standard 50mm lens. Having been around the circuits in an official capacity I knew how important it was not to intrude or get in the way just to get a picture. I would always stand back, watch what was going on and choose my moment carefully before snapping away at a driver sitting in a cockpit.

I always photographed during practice sessions and if I felt there was a tense moment for a driver or team I would walk away or shoot using a longer lens. The latter sometimes had the advantage of isolating the subject from the background and placing more emphasis on the driver's face or expression.

During a dry practice session on the Friday before the race Jackie made history by lapping the three-mile Silverstone circuit in just over 130mph when he recorded a lap of 1min 20.9 sec. For the race Jackie elected to drive the older MS10 Matra rather than the newer MS80 which he found rather a handful in the wet. A change of car meant starting on the back row of the grid but this did not deter him as he carved his way through the field to finish in third place behind Jochen Rindt who had overtaken him on lap 20.

In these two portraits standing back with a medium-to-long-focus lens allows items nearer the camera to provide a soft out of focus image around the driver and isolated Jackie Stewart from the background. Jackie also appears to be unaware of my camera's presence which helps with a more natural photograph.

Jackie Ickx – A Young and Promising Talent

Belgian Jackie Ickx, the son of a famous motor racing journalist, was 'discovered' by Ken Tyrell at the age of twenty-one following championship successes in saloon car racing. He was entered in Formula 2 events in 1966 and by 1968 he found himself driving for Ferrari.

In 1969 he was signed to drive for Jack Brabham's team and drove alongside the Australian maestro himself. Not that he needed to learn anything from the Australian world champion, as he was fast developing his own style and later in the season even managed a grand prix win in Germany over Jackie Stewart.

During Saturday morning practice for the race, I approached a very quiet and contemplative Jackie who did not mind a bit being photographed while mechanics made adjustments to his Brabham BT26. He demonstrated immaculate composure and concentration and I hope these qualities come over in the photographs.

He started the race alongside Jack Brabham on the front row of the grid and battled strongly with Piers Courage for second place until both were overtaken by the flying Jochen Rindt. He finished in a creditable third place and in that year went on to finish the world championship in second place behind Jackie Stewart,

Jackie Ickx has since retired from racing but became famous for his sports car racing performances including six wins at Le Mans.

Looking calm and relaxed before the practice session in which he puts the car on the front row of the grid at Silverstone.

After the portrait is taken Jackie relaxes and visualises the circuit while adjustments are made.

Jackie Ickx poses for the camera while the car is made ready for a practice lap.

Sir Jack Brabham OBE – The Gentleman Racer

For this event Jack Brabham was just days away from his 43rd birthday and had already been World Champion in 1959, 1960 and 1966 and here he was setting the pace with a pole position.

You would think that maturity, three world championships and being the first Formula 1 World Champion to win in a car carrying his own name would have been enough for this tough Australian. Not so for Jack Brabham whose style of driving was very characteristic of a man who would never give up.

Jack Brabham splashes his Brabham BT26 through a wet Woodcote Corner on his way to victory in the 21st Daily Express *trophy.*

The 21st *Daily Express* Trophy Race at Silverstone was no exception. After setting pole position he stormed away into the lead, leaving his fellow competitors floundering in his wake. Jochen Rindt however also had thoughts on the trophy and in a remarkable race was catching Jack Brabham at more than a second a lap. Catching Jack Brabham was one thing but getting past this man of experience was another. Within two laps of the finish Rindt had closed to within 12 seconds unaware of the fact that Brabham's car was running short of fuel. On the penultimate lap the Brabham's engine had cut out several times and the Rindt Lotus was closing in fast. I remember Jack Brabham almost coasting over the line to win the race with Jochen just 2.2 seconds behind.

A popular and worthy winner, Jack Brabham retired from racing in 1971 and returned to Australia having sold his share in the team to his partner and designer, Ron Tauranac. In 1979 he became the first racing driver to be knighted for services to motor racing.

A smiling Jack Brabham is congratulated on his pole position for the 21st Daily Express Trophy.

A winning smile and the winner's garland.

Jack Brabham Celebrates and I get a Scoop

It was one thing for me, an amateur photographer, to be given the opportunity of a press pass for major F1 events, but to stand on the winner's rostrum alongside one of motor racing's legendry heroes is quite another.

It happened at the 21st *Daily Express* Trophy race at Silverstone and was a moment I will always remember. The race was sensational with Jackie Stewart and Jochen Rindt storming through the field in wet conditions. Towards the end of the race Brabham's car was heard faltering and Jochen Rindt was closing in for second place. It was thought he may even catch and pass Jack Brabham on the last corner at Woodcote, just before the chequered flag.

I had rushed to a point between Woodcote and the finish line along with other press photographers. They were of course wielding their Nikons and I had my humble Praktica. I have to admit to feeling just a touch self conscious, particularly when I discovered I was standing next to Victor Blackman of the *Daily Express*. Discretion overcame valour and I remember moving behind him to allow 'the professional' a clearer view. Obviously this action would not have secured me a job on any newspaper and in the end I didn't get quite the picture I had in mind as Jack Brabham coasted across the finish line to win the race. However it was after all 'The *Daily Express* Trophy', so maybe I did the right thing.

After this scramble for a picture I rushed up to capture the prize giving. In those days it took place on a trailer behind a tractor. The Brabham BT26 was on the trailer and Jack was garlanded and presented with the trophy. As he was being interviewed by the late Raymond Baxter I was alongside the trailer with other press photographers. To my surprise, after the interview I was beckoned to go alongside them both, photographing the celebrating Jack Brabham at close quarters. A few other press photographers were also allowed on the trailer but space was at a premium and I remained one of the few to get such close images.

Jack Brabham holds the Daily Express *Trophy.*

David Piper's Lola at Copse in its resplendent green livery.

Lola T70 Sports Cars at Copse Corner

At each major Silverstone international the supporting races provided the opportunity of photographing cars in action and my favourites of that era were the Lola T70 sports cars.

With thunderous Chevrolet engines they were tremendous to watch and listen to. On this occasion I decided to capture the action from the inside of Copse Corner. There was only a small concrete wall, almost a ledge between you and the cars as they hurtled through Copse. Getting low with just a standard lens, the effect was quite dramatic with the car almost heading towards you.

It really was about as close as you could get to capturing the action and it was always a favourite spot for the motor sport photographers. I'm not sure such close photography would be allowed today.

I remember once asking one of the drivers if the close proximity of photographers at Copse ever put them off – "what photographers?" was his reply!

Opposite:
Brian Redman in Sid Taylor's Lola Chevrolet T70.
During the race Brian Redman was battling with Denny Hulme for the lead when an oil plug fell out of the gearbox of Hulme's car, covering the windscreen of Redman's Lola in oil. He managed to complete the race almost sightless and finished in second place.
The top of the wall can just be seen in the lower left of the picture.

Sports Car Race and Ecurie Bonnier

On such a dull day I had to concentrate my photography on the more colourful cars and teams on the grid. The yellow livery of Jo Bonnier's Ecurie Bonnier team provided the colour I needed.

The bright yellow Lolas stood out on the grid and were always immaculately prepared as indeed was Swedish owner and driver Jo Bonnier; when I photographed him he was approaching forty. His career had been varied rather than successful although wins for BRM at the Dutch GP in 1959 and for Porsche the following year in the Modena GP brought occasional fame. He also had successes in F2 including a spectacular win in the wet at a non-championship German GP and also in sports car racing with wins in the Nurburgring 1000kms and the Targa Florio. Finding his niche with sports cars, he took the European 2 Litre Championship in 1970.

During the 1960s however Jo Bonnier became the first leader of the newly formed Grand Prix Driver's Association and concentrated his efforts with others towards circuit design and safety within the sport.

It was at Le Mans in 1972 when ironically the career of Jo Bonnier came to an untimely end. His yellow Lola was in collision with a privately entered Ferrari and was launched over the crash barriers and into the surrounding trees. This experienced driver who had dedicated so much of his career to circuit safety had suddenly become a victim himself.

Opposite:
The characteristic look of concentration from Swedish driver Joachim (Jo) Bonnier as he checks his Lola T70.

Jo Bonnier's Lola T70 receives last minute checks on the grid.

Thruxton – The European Formula 2 Championship Comes to Hampshire

Following the closure of Goodwood, the British Automobile Racing Club (BARC) focused the traditional Easter Monday meeting on their new home circuit at Thruxton in Hampshire.

I was privileged to have been a flag marshal on the pits straight at Thruxton for the first Easter Monday meeting of 1968 and was able to witness the opening ceremony alongside my post.

It was a splendid opener for the circuit which had previously only held a member's race meeting just a few weeks before on the newly developed 2.356 mile circuit. The Easter Monday meeting saw 35,000 spectators and a terrific series of races for the Thruxton Trophy won by Jochen Rindt in Roy Winkelmann's Brabham BT23C Cosworth ahead of Jean-Pierre Beltoise in a work's Matra MS7 Cosworth and Derek Bell's Church Farm Racing Brabham BT23C Cosworth.

The celebrations were sobered however, by the untimely death of Jim Clark during a Formula 2 event at Hockenheim in Germany and who should have been entered for the race. Pole position on the grid was left open in his honour.

For 1969 however I was behind the camera and working for Agfa instead of the BARC. I knew Thruxton well and identified all the spots on the circuit from where my action shots would be taken. The European Formula 2 Championship brought with it a very colourful and continental atmosphere and in the spring sunshine Thruxton looked its best. I decided to make the most of both practice and race day and endeavoured to capture this exciting scene which only came to Thruxton once a year.

Clerk of the Course and Secretary of the Meeting, Grahame White, starts the 1969 BARC 200 Wills Trophy Race; the first round of the European Trophy for Formula 2 drivers.
The car nearest the camera is the Frank Williams Racing Brabham BT23C – FVA with Piers Courage at the wheel.

The starter's hands on the furled Union Jack as the cars assemble on the Thruxton grid.

On the grid for the 1969 European Formula 2 race at Thruxton.
Jochen Rindt in the Roy Winkelmann Racing Lotus 59B – FVA adjusts his helmet alongside the Matra Sports MS7 – FVA of Henri Pescarolo.

Johnny Servoz-Gavin's Matra MS7-FVA positioned on the grid.

On the Grid

The Formula 2 cars came from all over Europe and inevitably raced in their national colours which helped enormously in providing bright colourful imagery particularly on the grid.

There were always two heats and a final to this meeting which meant plenty of opportunity to capture images of cars lined up on the grid. Here I used a low viewpoint alongside the cars as they waited for the start.

The atmosphere before a race is something to be experienced as engines are revved. The noise is deafening and the drivers settle in the cockpit adjusting their gloves and goggles before all eyes are fixed on the starter.

The air is full of expectation as officials concentrate on the scene before them, marshals, observers and firemen ready themselves. The teams and mechanics watch expectantly from the pits, having entrusted their machinery to the driver all fingers are crossed, hoping intensely that it won't let their driver down.

Goggles are adjusted, fire marshals stand ready, the cars are positioned and all eyes are on the grid.

The View from the Grid

I'm sure I was significantly influenced by the images presented on screen in John Frankenheimer's epic film *Grand Prix*. When the cars were on the grid I remember those close up shots of drivers' hands on the wheel, rev counters with needles swinging, a view of the car in front and another of the car alongside. An occasional glimpse towards the driver on the next position and a quick glimpse of the instrument panel.

Before any race the cockpit becomes a very isolated environment as the driver sits motionless while mechanics make last minute checks and the inevitable crowds of well wishers and hangers on mill around the cars. Occasionally, a photographer will kneel beside a car and take a close-up of the driver but he is enclosed inside the car concentrating with only the sound of his own heartbeat for company.

The tension and build up before a race is what I have tried to convey in these images.

The silver helmet of Piers Courage – here Piers looks right towards the driver alongside him.

The familiar green helmet of Henri Pescarolo contrasts with the blue of the Matra Team.

The view on the grid behind Francois Cevert's Tecno.

Waiting for the Start

Just before the grid was cleared for the start I walked around the cars taking photographs of the drivers' hands on the wheels, the instruments and studies of concentration.

These were the final tense moments before the drivers were on their own jostling for position and establishing themselves on the circuit.

Just occasionally there would be one driver who would appear to be just too relaxed, but this may have been bravado or a touch of strategy against his competitors.

Race Car Imagery

Arriving at Thruxton early allowed me the opportunity to walk around the paddock in search of images. These primarily had to promote colour film and in this respect it was essential to capture photographs with strong colour, shape or light.

I therefore looked for shapes and sections of cars including the racing mirrors, engines and cockpit sections.

Shadow and light on the bodywork of the Scuderia Picchio Rossa Brabham BT23-FVA of Italian driver Enzo Corti.

The sparkle of a well prepared Cosworth FVA engine and bodywork of the Roy Winkelmann Lotus for Jochen Rindt.

Reflections in the racing mirrors were always a fascination for a photographer looking for images around the paddock.

Formula Vee driver Jenny Nadin relaxes during the lunch break.

Around the Paddock

The paddock was not only the place were the teams prepared their cars but a great place for people watching. Here I would wander around, camera at the ready trying to be as inconspicuous as possible and always searching for an interesting or amusing picture.

'Tyred legs' – a typical sixties' scene in the paddock.

Mini skirts and knee high boots were the fashion of the day and here they contrasted with the paddock surroundings of tool boxes and racing equipment.

The Ferrari Paddock

Opposite:

Paddock chat – Vittorio Brambilla on left and 'Tino' Brambilla third from left have discussions with a team mechanic.

The Ferrari paddock was always the place to search out a good picture and the Thruxton scene was no exception. In the morning as the cars were prepared for practice there would be much animated discussion between team members and drivers.

The familiar Ferrari red always photographed well and of course what international motor race would be complete without the legend of Ferrari and the famous prancing horse sign in the paddock.

The Ferrari Dino 166 V6 Formula 2 cars bore the name 'Dino' in honour of the son of Enzo Ferrari. Alfredo Ferrari had suffered ill health most of his life and died in 1956 at the age of twenty-four. Despite ill health Alfredo or Alfredino (little Alfredo) took an interest in the design of racing engines and was considering a V6 engine at the time of his death. His project was later finished by engineer Vittorio Jano. Enzo Ferrari dedicated the name Dino to his son's memory and the Formula 2 cars powered by the V6 engine carried the name Dino as also did a series of Ferrari Dino sports cars.

The 'Dino' badge on the Ferarri Dino 166 V6 F2 car of Ernesto 'Tino' Brambilla.

Ferrari and Ernesto 'Tino' Brambilla

At the chicane during practice I captured a number of images of Ernesto Brambilla in the Ferrari Dino 166 V6. This always seemed an extremely fast car and had been successful in the hands of Brambilla during the Argentinean series the previous winter. At Thruxton the car seemed very 'tail happy' and was certainly exciting to watch.

Brambilla had the reputation of being a notoriously hard racer and watching him execute the car in the fast downhill sections of Seagrave or up Woodham Hill and through the Club Chicane allowed me to get some wonderful action pictures. It also helped that the Dino in my opinion was an exceptionally beautiful racing car.

Ernesto or 'Tino' as he was more frequently known was the elder brother of Italian motorcycle racer, and later car racer, Vittorio Brambilla who frequently assisted him at events.

Despite successes in Formula 2 and offers of Formula 1 drives at Monza, Tino never realised a Formula 1 racing career.

At Thruxton 'Tino' brought the Dino home in ninth place in heat 2 and sixth place in the final round.

'Tino' Brambilla in discussions before the race.

Below left: Ernesto Brambilla's Ferrari Dino 166 V6 fitted with streamlined wheel covers at speed.

Below right: 'Tino' Brambilla edges the kerbs in the downhill section of Seagrave Corner.

Ernesto 'Tino' Brambilla exits the Thruxton Club Chicane during practice.

Ferrari and Clay Regazzoni

Ferrari was in attendance for the Thruxton meeting and with such obvious colour they were naturally one of the teams for me to focus on.

One car was driven by Clay Regazzoni who was raised in the Italian-speaking region of Ticino in Switzerland. Although holding a Swiss passport he was considered by Italians to be an Italian when driving for Ferrari.

Clay Regazzoni waits in the cockpit of his Ferrari in Thruxton's marshalling area before being released onto the circuit.

He raced in Formula 3 and Formula 2 in the late sixties and his rather uncompromising style of driving caused him to be involved in a number of racing incidents. However this appeared to be overlooked when he was invited to drive for Ferrari in Formula 1 in 1970. Regazzoni cemented his Ferrari relationship by winning the Italian Grand Prix in Monza, finishing the world championship in third place behind his team mate Jackie Ickx and Jochen Rindt who became motor racing's first posthumous world champion after his tragic crash during practice for the race.

Regazzoni's Formula 1 career continued with BRM before returning to Ferrari again in 1974. Several Formula 1 wins followed as did drives with other teams including Ensign, Shadow and Williams. While driving for Ensign in the USA a broken brake pedal caused the car to crash heavily. Clay Regazzoni suffered severe back injuries which left him paralysed from the waist down.

Despite his disability he pioneered causes for disabled people, commentated on the sport and even took part in sports car races using specially adapted hand controls. He also took part in the gruelling Paris-Dakar Rally.

Clay Regazzoni died in an Italian motorway accident in 2006.

Clay Regazzoni in the Ferrari Dino 166 V6 steers through the Thruxton chicane on his way to an overall tenth place.

Ferrari and Derek Bell

Ferrari had entered a full team of cars including one for Derek Bell, who once lived near the Goodwood circuit in Sussex. Despite a spirited performance, Derek Bell's Ferrari suffered fuel pressure problems on lap 23 of the final race.

Derek Bell began his racing career in 1964 graduating to Formula 3 and in 1967 managed seven wins in the Formula 3 season. This success allowed him to graduate to Formula 2 with his stepfather's Church Farm Racing Team.

Bell is an experienced racer having driven for such teams as Ferrari, McLaren, Surtees, Williams and Tecno but it is success in sports car racing for which he is best known. He has won Le Mans five times and the Daytona 24 Hours three times. His record breaking wins with Porsche and co-driver Jackie Ickx have nominated them both as the most successful sports car driving team in motor racing history.

Derek Bell was awarded the MBE for services to motor sport in 1986 and has since pioneered the winning Bentley team at Le Mans as consultant. Frequently driving in historic events he has also partnered his son Justin in the Le Mans 24 Hour races of 1992 and 1996.

Derek Bell.

Derek Bell guides the Ferrari through the fast downhill section of Seagrave Corner.

The Ferrari Dino 166 V6 of Derek Bell in the Thruxton chicane.

Francois Cevert at speed in the Tecno where the blurred colours of the background combine with the Tecno team colours.

Francois Cevert and the Colourful Tecno

For a photographer in search of colour at an international race meeting I needed only to have focused on the Tecno team cars and the helmet of their driver, Francois Cevert. He was himself a very colourful and charismatic character. The son of a Paris jeweller, he was also an accomplished pianist and the brother in law of Jean-Pierre Beltoise, a fellow Formula 1 and 2 driver.

After winning the French Formula 3 Championship in 1968 Francois joined the Tecno Formula 2 team for 1969. During this season Jackie Stewart found Francois to be a strong competitor and mentioned to Ken Tyrell to keep his eye on this young Frenchman. However, early in the 1970 season Ken Tyrell invited Francois to join his Formula 1 team alongside defending world champion Jackie Stewart. Thus he became the protégé of Jackie Stewart and a very supportive team driver.

Throughout the 1971 season the team were a force to be reckoned with culminating in Francois securing a win at the season-ending US Grand Prix at Watkins Glen.

1972 was not a good year for Tyrell but Francois did take second place in the Le Mans 24 hour race with New Zealander Howden Ganley in a Matra Simca.

The following season saw Tyrell back with vengeance and their two drivers Jackie Stewart and Francois Cevert working well together, allowing Stewart to clinch his third world championship at Monza. The two drivers had developed a close relationship and were extremely good friends off the track as well as in the team environment.

During the 1973 season Jackie had secretly decided to retire from racing after the final grand prix staged in the USA at Watkins Glen in October. Sadly Francois Cevert was killed during practice for the race while battling for pole position with Ronnie Peterson. Stewart immediately announced his retirement from racing and the Tyrell team withdrew from the 1973 US Grand Prix. The final race of the season was to have been Jackie Stewart's 100th grand prix.

Francois Cevert pulls down his face mask to have a chat while waiting to be released on to the track.

On the grid Francois prepares himself in the cockpit of the Tecno Racing Tecno 68 – FVA.

Paddock Chat – Graham Hill and Jackie Stewart

Scenes around the paddock could always be relied upon to provide interest and the Thruxton paddock with so many international drivers in attendance was no exception.

With a medium telephoto lens (180mm Soligor) I was able to stay reasonably detached from the subjects in order to draw more attention to them.

Here I came across Graham Hill and Jackie Stewart seemingly in deep conversation. Jackie was wearing his usual black corduroy cap from under which his fashionable growth of hair flowed.

As was inevitably the case with Graham Hill around, the subject matter soon became light hearted and Jackie's hair appeared to become the focus of attention, even more so when Piers Courage entered into the spirit of things.

Such moments indicate the light-hearted camaraderie among drivers in those days.

Graham Hill and Jackie Stewart in conversation before the race.

Jackie's hairstyle and cap appear to become the subject matter.

A re-arrangement of the cap from Jackie and Piers Courage joins in.

Graham Hill

Thruxton's European Formula 2 Championship meeting was always the season opener based around the Easter calendar and attracted a number of Formula 1 drivers racing alongside some aspiring non-graded drivers. The races for which 30 cars were entered were run in two 15 lap heats and a 50 lap final.

Graham Hill and Jochen Rindt were entered in brand new Lotus 59Bs with the inevitable Cosworth engines. The cars were entered by industrialist Roy Winkelmann and managed by Alan Rees.

These images of Graham Hill were captured as he prepared for the first heat in which he came third behind the Matra MS7s of Jackie Stewart and Jean-Pierre Beltoise; having recovered from a spin at the Campbell, Cobb and Seagrave complex.

During the practice session I decided to take some action shots as the cars approached the complex of Campbell, Cobb and Seagrave, having accelerated through Allard and up the slight rise to the complex. Here I was able to achieve an uncomplicated background with only the airfield and green fields of Hampshire in the background

Graham Hill's Lotus was performing well but despite a third place in heat 1 only managed to get as far as the first corner at Allard in the final due to a broken clutch.

Thruxton's high speed corners were ideally suited for Formula 2 cars and the drivers revelled in the circuit.

Graham Hill prepares for a practice session driving the Roy Winkelmann Racing-entered Lotus 59B FVA.

Graham Hill approaches the Thruxton complex in the new Lotus 59B during heat 1.

Graham Hill steps into the cockpit of the Lotus 59B.
During the race Graham managed to spin the Lotus at the complex
when his hand hit on his thighs in the very tight cockpit. This was
later modified to allow more hand room and manoeuvrability.

Bette Hill carries out her timing duties in the Thruxton pits.

Henri Pescarolo

The green helmet of the bearded Henri Pescarolo talking to team mate Jean-Pierre Beltoise on the grid.

Henri Pescarolo is a driver from the Calvados region of northern France and gave up being a medical student to become a racing driver. His distinctive green helmet contrasted colourfully with the French blue Matras with which he had so much success.

He went on to drive for Matra in F2 during 1968 and 1969 in addition to three Formula 1 drives, competing a full season for Matra in 1970, collecting a third place at Monaco. He later drove for Williams and managed a fourth place in the 1971 British Grand Prix.

It was Henri's change to sports car racing that brought him most success with wins for Matra at Le Mans in 1972, 1973 and 1974. He won Le Mans again in 1984 but in a Porsche and the Daytona 24 hours in 1991.

At Thruxton in April 1969 he was second in heat 2 and fourth overall in the final.

It is astonishing to recall that little more than a week after these photographs were taken Henri was seriously injured in a high speed accident at Le Mans when testing the new Matra MS640 Prototype. The car flipped and burst into flames from which he suffered severe burns.

Undeterred, he has become a significant sports car racer, rally driver and now team owner with Pescarolo Sport.

He is also a renowned aviator, when in 1984 with Patrick Fourticq he set the fastest recorded crossing of the Atlantic from New York to Paris in a single-engined aircraft.

The Matra MS7 is steered through the Thruxton chicane.

Henri Pescarolo powers the Matra MS7 through Thruxton's sweeping curves.

Johnny Servoz-Gavin

Born George-Francis, "Johnny" Servoz-Gavin came from Grenoble and earned himself the reputation of being something of a playboy. He certainly loved the good life and was rarely seen without a smile on his face.

However, he also had a tremendous talent as a racing driver winning the French Formula 3 title in 1966 and in the year these photographs were taken he won the 1969 European Formula 2 Championship for Matra.

After Jackie Stewart sustained a wrist injury in 1968 Johnny was asked to join Ken Tyrell's Matra team. He led the Monaco Grand Prix from the start with a superb drive over three laps until the inevitable Monaco armco managed to get in his way with a resultant broken driveshaft. At Monza however he brought the car home in a very creditable second place.

He was also signed to join Jackie Stewart in Tyrell's March Team but an off road incident in a jeep caused him to be struck in the face with a branch causing damage to his eyesight. For a while he continued to race but decided to retire after concerns about his vision.

Johnny Servoz-Gavin's Matra and mechanic in the Thruxton marshalling area before the race; in the background is the Ferrari Dino of 'Tino' Brambilla who is out of the car and in conversation with Piers Courage in the Frank Williams' Brabham.

For a while Johnny lived on a house boat until 1982 when he suffered severe burns after a gas bottle exploded. Surgeon's fought to save his life three times during the course of an operation. After recovering he spent much time travelling around the Mediterranean in a horse drawn caravan. Johnny Servoz-Gavin died in May 2006.

A cheery smile from Johnny Servoz-Gavin before the race at Thruxton in which he secured fourth in heat 2 after a considerable challenge with the tail-sliding Ferrari of Ernesto 'Tino' Brambilla. In the final the Frenchman's Matra finished overall in fifth place behind his team mates Henri Pescarolo, Jean-Pierre Beltoise and Jackie Stewart.

Jackie Stewart in the 'T' car Matra MS7 during practice for the F2 race; here he guides the car through Seagrave Corner. Note the name on the 'T' car is for Johnny Servoz-Gavin.

Jackie Stewart – Matra

Matra entered no less than four cars for the European Formula 2 Championship opener at Thruxton for drivers Jackie Stewart, Jean-Pierre Beltoise, Henri Pescarolo and Johnny Servoz-Gavin. In fact that is the way in which they all finished the final race behind the winning Lotus 59B of Jochen Rindt.

With the resplendent blue livery of the Matra MS7s they were the ideal subject for my camera and Agfa's CT18 colour film.

During practice I took some photographs at the fast downhill Seagrave Corner where I spotted Jackie Stewart at the wheel of Jonnny Servoz-Gavin's car.

In the paddock before the race I also found Jackie's helmet with the famous tartan band resting on the wing of Graham Hill's Lotus, but that's how it was in those days all very relaxed and friendly.

During heat 1, Jackie Stewart dominated, winning from team mate Jean-Pierre Beltoise and Graham Hill in third place with the Roy Winkelmann Lotus 59B.

However, the final saw the early dominance of the Matras with Stewart, Beltoise and Perscarolo heading straight into the lead. They were followed closely by Kurt Ahrens, Piers Courage, and privateer Bill Ivy in his first ever Formula 2 race with Clay Regazzoni in the first of the Ferraris close behind.

All four of these contenders retired before the end of the 50 lap final. However Piers Courage did manage to take the Matra of Beltoise before a puncture intervened.

Jochen Rindt in the Lotus 59B raced through the field from being eighth on the grid and eventually took Jackie for the lead on lap 19.

The characteristic tartan band on Jackie Stewart's helmet resting on the wing of Graham Hill's Lotus.

Jackie Stewart's Matra passes through the Thruxton chicane.

Jochen Rindt – 'The King of F2'

In 1968 Jochen Rindt became the first driver to win a Formula 2 race at Thruxton after the BARC moved to the Hampshire circuit from Goodwood.

For the 1969 Easter Monday meeting Jochen Rindt was in one of Roy Winkelmann's brand new Lotus 59B cars. Right from the start the car looked on form and indeed so did its driver. He was teamed with Gaham Hill and with their new cars seemingly well sorted they looked to be a formidable force against the Matras, Tecnos, Brabhams and Ferraris.

The advent of wings and the more powerful FVA engines combined to reduce Thruxton lap times by over two seconds and Jochen Rindt was soon establishing his prowess with a 1 min 13.2 sec lap of the 2.356 mile circuit.

In heat 2 Jochen established a firm lead ahead of the rest of the field until a puncture forced him into the pits. This left Piers Courage to take first ahead of Henri Pescarolo in a Matra and Ernesto Brambilla's Ferrari.

In the 50 lap final however Jochen found himself back on row 8 of the grid as a result of the heat 2 puncture and things did not improve when on the warm up lap his rev counter failed and his team mate Graham Hill experienced clutch problems at the start.

Although unable to judge his engine's revs Jochen powered through the field in a dynamic style. Although Jackie Stewart had taken control of the race in his Matra even his skill and professionalism was not enough to hold off the charging Rindt who caught and overtook the Matra under braking at the chicane on lap 19. The crowd were on their feet and the atmosphere electric as Jochen pulled away at a second a lap. At the finish Jochen was more than half a minute ahead of Jackie Stewart's Matra. It was a phenomenal performance and a memorable race which made Jochen Rindt Thruxton's 'King of Formula 2'.

Jochen Rindt in the immaculately prepared Roy Winkelmann Racing Lotus 59B exits the Thruxton chicane.

Commentator Tony Vlassopulo interviews Jochen Rindt after a presentation for achieving fastest lap.

The characteristic driving style of Jochen Rindt is displayed at the complex in the Lotus 59B.

Jochen Rindt – Congratulations

After witnessing such an epic Formula 2 race, I just had to get myself into position to photograph Jochen Rindt as he brought the Lotus 59B back to the grid after the slowing down lap.

As Jochen brought the car to a standstill and emerged from the car, the applause from the crowd was rapturous and as he stood beside the Lotus to remove his goggles and helmet I managed to get the first shots of the Thruxton winner.

Almost immediately his team mate Graham Hill and Jochen's wife Nina arrived on the scene to congratulate him and I was able to photograph this happy scene as both drivers swapped stories of their race.

I was then off to the winner's rostrum to secure my position for more celebration photographs.

Removing his goggles after winning the race.

Graham Hill and Jochen's wife Nina are the first to congratulate Jochen.

The winner – Jochen Rindt.

"Well is this what I've actually raced for?"

Winning his Thruxton Formula 2 hat trick – 1970 in a Lotus 69 Cosworth FVA.

Jochen Rindt Celebrates

There was no doubt in anyone's mind that we had all witnessed one of those rare and remarkable drives which happen in motor racing from time to time.

It was a popular win for the Austrian who seemed remarkably composed and even had time to pull a face at the somewhat small size of the 'Wills' trophy he was presented with; however it was soon smiles all round when it was filled with champagne.

It was a superb end to a classic race and one which I was very privileged to have witnessed and photographed.

Jochen was without doubt the 'King of Formula 2' but his wins began back in 1962 when his Alfa Romeo Giulia Ti outperformed 3 litre cars in saloon car racing. Other wins included the 1965 Austrian Sports Car Grand Prix at Zeltweg with a Ferrari 250LM, the Prix du Tyrol in Innsbruck with a Fiat Abarth 2000 and the Le Mans 24 Hour Race with American Masten Gregory in a Ferrari 250LM. With this win he became the first Austrian to win at Le Mans.

Jochen had a reputation for being a hard driver and equally hard on his cars. He certainly experienced moments of unreliability and Formula 1 victories did not come his way until joining Team Lotus in 1968. His first F1 victory was the USA Grand prix at Watkins Glen, the event which was overshadowed by the accident to his team mate Graham Hill who was out of action for several months with two broken legs.

The 1969 season saw some outstanding drives but 1970 saw wins for Team Lotus in the 72 design at Monaco, Holland, France, Britain and Germany. Despite these successes and with a world championship a distinct possibility, Jochen had made a decision to retire from racing at the end of the season.

During practice for the 1970 Italian Grand Prix his Lotus 72 went out of control under braking at the Parabolica, crashing at high speed into and under the barriers. The 28 year old died on the way to hospital.

The victor's smile.

The taste of victory.

At the time of his accident Jochen had won 5 of the year's 10 grand prix races, his world championship lead was unchallengeable and he became motor racing's first posthumous world champion.

In 1971 the BARC presented the Jochen Rindt Memorial Trophy to his former team mate Graham Hill following his Formula 2 win. Jochen had always excelled at Thruxton and the trophy became a fitting tribute to this great driver and world champion.

Jackie Stewart – After the Race

Although it had been Jochen Rindt's win I also focused the camera on Jackie Stewart who had brought his Matra MS7 home in second place with team mate Jean-Pierre Beltoise in third. Both had succumbed to the unbelievable performance of Jochen Rindt but they had unquestionably put up a brave fight.

It was reported in *Motor Sport* that this had been the first time Rindt had beaten Jackie. In previous races one or the other had retired before there had been a conclusive result.

Jackie Stewart after an epic drive against Jochen Rindt.

Jackie Stewart after a hard fought second place to Jochen Rindt.

A victory tour around the circuit with second place Jackie Stewart and Matra team-mate Jean-Pierre Beltoise who took third place.

Thruxton – RAC Sports Car Championship 1969

Lola T70s Dominate a Colourful Grid

It was spectacular, colourful and a noisy race with the sports cars at Thruxton entered for the Wills Embassy Trophy Race. The powerful cars certainly used the full high speed potential of the Thruxton circuit. With the Lola's thunderous 5 litre engines powering the cars through Village, Brooklands and up Woodham Hill towards the Club Chicane it was an incredible sight.

Once again the Thruxton paddock and grid provided some colourful images of the cars being prepared and lined up for the race.

Bonnier and Redman in their Lola T70 Mk 111Bs had a magnificent duel for most of the 25 laps with the experienced Bonnier holding the lead for 20 laps before Redman slipped by to take the lead and the race.

The grid lined up for the RAC Sports Car Race.

Paul Hawkins Lola T70 on the Thruxton grid.

David Piper's Lola T70 in his customary green livery which finished in fourth place.

The Ecurie Bonnier Team working on their Lola T70 to be driven by Jo Bonnier.

Jo Bonnier on the grid.

Brian Redman in Sid Taylor's Lola T70 takes the inside line into the Club Chicane against Jo Bonnier's yellow Lola. Redman went on to win the race with Bonnier a close second behind.

Martini International 300 Trophy Race – Silverstone May 1969

Images in the Wet

This event was probably the wettest I had experienced and here I was being expected by Agfa's advertising department to capture some bright colourful pictures.

I decided that it was best to not only capture the brightest and most colourful cars on the track as they made their way around the circuit but also to look for alternative shots around the pits and paddock.

By 1pm the Martini International Formula 3 race was lining up at the circuit entrance opposite Woodcote Corner. I wandered over in search of images and could not resist the scene of Swedish driver Rolf Tellsten sitting in the cockpit of his Brabham holding an umbrella in an attempt to protect himself from the elements while his companion blocked her ears from the sound of cars racing towards the chequered flag in the previous race. It has since proved to be one of the most popular pictures I captured that day.

Headlights ablaze, Australian Paul Hawkins battles with the British weather in his Lola T70.

Opposite:
Keeping the driver and cockpit dry is the priority of the day.

95

Chris Craft and the Smile of Success

The Martini International 300 Trophy, organised by the Aston Martin Owner's Club was destined to be a real high powered affair with the mighty Lola T70s fighting it out with the infamous Ford GT40s. With many of the cars harbouring engines approaching 5000cc the racing promised to be fast and furious but in true British style, it rained and rained.

The race became a tedious, soggy procession enlivened occasionally with the odd spin. The weather even took its toll on the cars. Out of 27 starters only 19 finished.

Chris Craft won the race in the orange coloured Tech Speed Racing Lola T70. He wrestled the 4965cc car through 65 soggy Silverstone laps at an average speed of 85.28 mph. Later in the day, on a drying circuit, the less powerful historic cars managed a win at an average speed of 98.47 mph

Chris Craft's victory smile may well have been one of relief after battling 65 laps of Silverstone in extremely wet conditions.

Chris Craft's Lola splashes its way to victory in the Martini International of 1969.

A Ferrari 625 from 1957 through Copse Corner.

Historic Racing Cars – Silverstone May 1969

Ferraris and Maseratis – The Power and the Glory

Again Silverstone's Copse Corner was the venue for some photography of motor racing's classics. The cars during the 1950s were 'my stars' and as a child I well remember my Dinky Toy Maserati 250F, Talbot Lago, Vanwall and Cooper Bristol. Now I was able to photograph those very cars racing.

I simply loved these cars. The sight, sound and smells were quite different from their modern counterparts. The suspension designs were obviously less sophisticated and made the cars quite a handful in corners and with cut away cockpits the drivers could be seen wrestling at the wheel.

P. Bergel's Maserati 1956 250F at Copse Corner.

Saloon Car Racing

The Mini Years

During the 1960s the Minis reigned supreme in saloon car racing. Their phenomenal performance and handling enabled them to outperform much larger engined cars. If the driver was brave enough it was possible at some circuits to use the cars' incredible handling characteristics to minimise braking and therefore keep up momentum. Some drivers would even claim to dispense with braking altogether! Christabel Carlisle, John Aley, John Love, John Whitmore, John Handley, John Rhodes, Steve Neal and Gordon Spice were among the chief Mini racing exponents of the era.

The art of Mini racing was clearly demonstrated with beautifully turned out cars from the John Cooper stable with their distinctive white bands down the bonnet.

The works 1275cc Mini Coopers in the Silverstone paddock.

The Mini Years – The Britax Cooper Downton Team

One of the most colourful teams to race Minis in the late 1960s was the Britax Cooper Downton Team with their 1275 S versions for Gordon Spice and Steve Neal. As subjects for my Agfa colour film assignment they were ideal.

Gordon Spice at Thruxton's Club Chicane.

Mrs Gordon Spice wearing distinctive head gear as part of the Britax Cooper Downton pit crew.

Gordon Spice on the Thruxton grid.

The Mini Years - British Leyland Works Team

John Handley and John Rhodes were always sideways drifters as Mini racers and their British Leyland team cars were immaculately prepared in their red and white livery.

John Rhodes drifts through Copse Corner at Silverstone – 1969.

John Handley at the Club Chicane – Thruxton 1969.

John Rhodes on the Thruxton grid – 1969.

More Images from the Saloon Car Racing Days of the Late 1960s

Club racing and Chris Inch angles his 850cc Mini through the Thruxton chicane during the circuit's first club meeting organised by the BARC on 17th March 1968.

Fast and furious around Paddock Bend at Brands Hatch with Frank Gardner in the Alan Mann Racing twin cam Ford Escort leading the field of Ford Falcons, Lotus Cortinas and Escorts in the Guards Trophy Race – July 1968.

Club racing at London's Crystal Palace with Roger Taylor's Dagenham Motors-entered Ford Escort leading a 'gaggle' of Minis, Escorts and Anglias through the parkland setting – September 1968.

Frank Gardner exits the Thruxton chicane on three wheels with the Alan Mann Twin-Cam Ford Escort – 1969.

22nd RAC British Grand Prix – Silverstone July 1969

Colour and Fashion

July saw another race and another grand prix. Agfa as usual had arranged the necessary passes and I was on my way to Silverstone yet again. I was beginning to get used to this life and I have to say feeling quite at home in it, no longer being quite so intimidated by the press boys and determined to concentrate on getting the shots.

For this event I had been briefed to concentrate on the colourful scenes behind the racing, the mechanics, personalities, drivers and their wives all had to be captured as well as anything fashionable or trendy. After all this was the last year of the 'swinging sixties' and who knew what the 'seventies' had in store?

As soon as I arrived at the circuit on practice day I headed for the paddock and pits. The day was bright and sunny which helped and for just a while my focus was taken away from the cars and drivers as I searched for those colourful and 'sixties' fashion images.

In the late sixties advertising came to motor racing – and not just on the cars!!

Opposite: *A container in one hand and handbag in the other – a typical paddock scene in 1969.*

Around the Paddock

Looking back through my programme for this event it is interesting to note that entrance for practice on each of the two days was 10 shillings (50p), rising to £1 on race day. A further 50 shillings (£2.50) would secure a grandstand seat and an additional 30 shillings (£1.50) would provide spectators with entrance to the paddock where a close up view of the cars and drivers was always possible. It is also interesting to compare the paddock at Silverstone in 1969 with the clean, well-lit garages within the pits that Formula 1 teams enjoy today.

In 1969 teams parked their transporters and race cars behind the pits. The paddock and pits were separated by a small fence with only foot access at strategic points. This meant teams having to work on their cars in the open on a gravel surface and when ready for practice or race, the cars were manoeuvred into a marshalling area at the end of the pits near the exit to Woodcote Corner, on the inside of the circuit. Cars were then released onto the track or pit lane as appropriate at allotted times.

A mechanic's tools of his trade.

Gold Leaf Team Lotus mechanics in discussion.

Opposite: *The red, white and gold colours of the Gold Leaf Team Lotus cars; Graham Hill's car sports No 1 for the reigning World Champion. Advertising on cars and major team sponsorship were relatively new in 1969.*

The evocative sign of the prancing horse on the side of a Ferrari transporter.

F1 cockpit and the prancing horse emblem.

Ferrari Red

The Agfa brief was firmly established in my mind: "It's a colourful sport, capture the atmosphere", John Shire had said to me and the images were of course all about promoting a colour film.

It was one thing to be out on the track photographing the action but the cars themselves presented images of colour and of course none more so than Ferrari. The resplendent red of Ferrari and the famous prancing horse emblem captured the excitement and glamour of grand prix racing.

A plan soon evolved and at each meeting before the start of practice or during lunch, I would seek out the cars in the paddock and take some images, working around each car as best I could in sometimes crowded and compact areas, always taking care not to get in the way of the mechanics.

Ferrari's Engineer 'Borzari'.

It wasn't long before I became a regular feature among some of the guys who would quickly polish a car and stand to one side while I took the images. They were obviously very proud of their work and compared to this day and age I can't believe how relaxed they all were. In today's grand prix scene I am certain such images would be very difficult to obtain. Even Ferrari's chief mechanic at the time 'Borzari' was pleased to pose for the camera in the Silverstone paddock while making adjustments to Derek Bell's car.

Ferrari Red.

John Bolster

No British Grand Prix was complete without the sight of commentator and motoring writer John Bolster, always sporting his check suits and a deerstalker hat. This colourful and flamboyant character always had a cheery and exuberant personality and was a walking encyclopaedia of motor racing facts and figures.

To me John was always part of the scene and epitomized the sport with his excited humour and infectious enthusiasm. In fact I perhaps owe more to John Bolster than I care to admit for my passion for the sport. As a school boy in the fifties I was once presented with John Bolster's book as a school prize and I will always remember the black and white television broadcasts on Saturdays with commentaries by Raymond Baxter and John Bolster. The Raymond Baxter commentaries were of course full of technical fact and delivered with that sublime Englishness that only Raymond Baxter could muster but when those famous words "and now over to John Bolster in the pits" were aired even a dull race suddenly became exciting. In his race to get out the words the 'rs' were dropped and statements were often repeated but even though I was at home some 150 miles from Silverstone, I was there living every moment.

John Bolster of course was most famous for his 'Bloody Mary' special, the twin engined JAP powered hill climb and sprint car which started life in 1929. The final version had four engines mounted in the light wooden chassis, the engines were run on a methanol-based fuel and I believe Bolster once described 'BM' as having as much liking for alcohol as her owner! I recall he also described his performances at the Prescott hill climb as being improved if somewhat 'erratically' by a glass or two of Beaujolais during lunch.

John was an outstanding race driver with many a story to tell but his racing career was curtailed when driving an ERA in the 1949 British Grand Prix when he was badly injured in a crash at Silverstone.

One of motor racing's characters and certainly one I will never forget, John Bolster died in 1984.

During morning practice I spotted John Bolster in the pits so engrossed in lap times and swatting up race numbers that he was completely oblivious to his surroundings!!

Drivers' Wives and Girlfriends – The Doghouse Club

As I have said many times, motor racing in the sixties was a very friendly, almost family affair. The drivers would compete against each other on the track, sometimes holding absolutely nothing back; after all they were racers with race wins and championships at stake. Off the track they were far more relaxed and sociable.

The wives and girlfriends were also very much in evidence supporting their man and doing a very useful job of work with the team. On this practice morning for the grand prix, the seats above the pits were occupied by the girls carrying out their time-keeping and lap-scoring duties.

Time-keeping was a highly concentrated activity in those days. There were no electronic timing devices; everything was done with manual stopwatches and a lap chart. It was necessary to chart every lap and keep a watchful eye on the circuit; it required a high level of concentration and accuracy in all weathers and in all conditions.

Racing was far more dangerous in those days than it is now and if there was an accident, they were there to support each other. Most said they would rather be at the circuit knowing what was going on, or be involved with the activity rather than being at home wondering what was happening.

Graham Hill's wife Bette was one of the racing wives who, together with others, formed 'The Doghouse Club' in 1962. After getting fed up with their husbands leaving dinner tables and sitting around in bars talking shop, the wives got together and formed their own club.

As The Doghouse Club grew, the ladies organised events for charity, with many of the drivers adding their support. They also formed their own benevolent fund in support of any family who might be affected by the death or injury of any driver, mechanic or journalist or indeed anyone connected with the sport.

Stopwatch in hand, a lap chart is examined.

Bette Hill on left with Lynne Oliver, wife of Jackie Oliver during practice for the British Grand Prix at Silverstone.

Nina Rindt, wife of Jochen, keeps an eye on Woodcote Corner from her seat in the pits.

Opposite:
A lighthearted moment for Jackie Stewart's wife Helen.

These pictures show a somewhat serious Graham Hill who spent more time in the pits during practice than on the track; the frustration and disappointment shows clearly in the World Champion's face. At times even the best of drivers can have the worst of luck.

Graham Hill's Frustrating Weekend

Graham Hill, the forty-year-old Londoner had become world champion for the second time in 1968 and as the current World Champion it was obviously important for me to get some shots of this charismatic and fun-loving driver.

Race driver, husband and father, Graham Hill was very much a family man who had started in motor racing the hard way as a mechanic, desperately seeking drives in Lotus sports cars whenever he could. He first drove in Formula 1 in 1958, the year Lotus decided to enter grand prix racing. In 1962 he became World Champion for the first time when driving a V8 BRM and in 1967 he rejoined Lotus as team mate to the legendary Jim Clark. Following Jimmy's untimely death in 1968 during a F2 event at Hockenheim in Germany, Graham drove to victory in the world championship at a time when morale was very low for the team.

Graham always proved to be the man to have around when morale was low. His witty sense of humour and mischievous sense of fun was something for which Graham Hill will always be remembered.

For this meeting I kept an eye on the World Champion and made sure I was always somewhere near the Lotus pit and paddock area, ready to take some images whenever they presented themselves.

During Friday morning practice I took some portraits of Graham in the cockpit while having adjustments made to the car. It was clear things were not going too well, in fact it was not his weekend and I think the frustration clearly shows in his face.

On the Friday only a few practice laps were possible in a borrowed Lotus 49. The car suffered from trouble with the wheel bearings, then a broken water pipe and finally no fuel pressure. Saturday saw the car having an engine change and the result was the World Champion having to start well down the grid in twelfth place. However Graham did manage a spirited duel with Piers Courage and Jo Siffert which lasted most of the race.

Eventually, however, he ran out of petrol in the closing laps; not the best of weekends for a reigning World Champion.

Graham Hill Starts Rumours in the Silverstone Paddock

While being around the Lotus pits waiting for images I soon realised that not being at Silverstone on the previous practice day I had missed some good pictures and a good story

On the first day of practice no cars were available for Graham Hill and Jochen Rindt during the morning session. So somewhat bored with life Graham went on walkabout among the other teams and found quite the reverse situation in the Brabham camp – two cars and no drivers. Jack Brabham had injured his foot and Jackie Ickx was delayed getting to Silverstone.

Brabham designer and team boss Ron Tauranac offered Graham the chance to drive one of their cars. Graham didn't need asking twice. After a couple of laps he entered the pits in the Brabham and suggested one or two suspension setting changes and eventually got the car going quite quickly. This of course meant speculation and rumour was rife around the Silverstone paddock but of course it was all unfounded.

Just imagine that ever happening in the world of Formula 1 today.

Graham Hill and Ron Tauranac in discussion again but this time much later in May 1971 when Graham drove a Motor Racing Developments Brabham in the GKN-Daily Express International Trophy meeting.

Opposite: *Graham Hill waits in the cockpit of his Lotus 49B while adjustments are made. This shot was taken from above the Silverstone pits, a good location for cockpit shots.*

Graham Hill

Although the 1969 British Grand Prix was not a huge success for the World Champion it was the USA Grand Prix of that year which nearly claimed him when driving the four wheel drive Lotus 63. A puncture caused the Lotus to fly off the track; Hill was thrown out of the cockpit breaking both legs. He had not fastened his belts adequately having previously push-started the car following a spin in which the car had stalled. This was probably a blessing in disguise as the Lotus was completely wrecked in the crash.

Graham Hill was a strong and determined character and returned to grand prix racing in the South African Grand Prix in March 1970, finishing in sixth place.

Hill continued to show his versatility with a win in the 1972 Le Mans 24 Hour race with Henri Pescarolo driving a Matra MS670 and he became the first driver ever to win the Indy 500, the F1 World Championship and the Le Mans 24 Hours race – motor racing's sensational triple crown.

In 1973 Graham formed his own team in the name of Embassy Hill Racing and this continued until 1975 when he announced his retirement from driving handing over to Tony Brise, an up-and-coming driver to front the Embassy Hill Racing team on the grand prix circuits.

However, in November 1975 Graham Hill was killed when his Piper Aztec crashed in foggy conditions on a golf course in North London. With him were driver Tony Brise and other members of the team. They had been flying home from a test session in the south of France.

During his career Graham Hill had taken part in 176 grands prix and won 14 races, achieved wins at Le Mans and the Indianapolis 500 in addition to winning two Formula 1 World Championships. Above all he was a gentleman racer with a sense of humour and a true ambassador for the sport.

Graham Hill, Silverstone, March 1969.

This was the last photograph I ever took of Graham Hill driving his own team car, at Brands Hatch in April 1974.

Jochen Rindt and Jackie Stewart Battle it out for £100

Early in the 1969 season it was evident that Jackie Stewart in the Matra MS80 and Jochen Rindt in the Lotus 49B were the main contenders for the championship.

Both teams were experimenting with four wheel drive technology, therefore a mixture of cars was available to both drivers. Rindt had the Lotus 49B and the four wheel drive 63 and of course Stewart had the successful Matra MS80 and the new four wheel drive version; both teams' cars were powered by V8 Cosworth engines.

The Friday afternoon practice session was a two hour affair split into four continuous 30 minute sessions with £100 as a prize for the fastest lap established within each half hour. First to set the lap was Jackie Stewart with a 1min 21.1 sec; he then sat back in the pits and waited to see what the opposition would produce. In reality the only opposition was Jochen Rindt in the Lotus 49B. During the second session Jackie Stewart was out with a resounding 1min 20.6 sec (averaging 130.7 mph); Rindt could only manage 1 min 21.

Then Jackie got behind the wheel of the MS80. I was quite near the Tyrell pit at the time and detected an air of confidence and remember thinking this is going to be some lap. After the initial warm up I remember Jackie coming past the pits with the car sounding really wound up. It was quite a sight, the atmosphere electric.

Coming through Woodcote the car appeared to loose control, spinning from a 135mph corner, reducing speed rapidly and hitting the banking in front of the grandstands. Stewart emerged unhurt but the car was severely damaged. It soon became apparent that a loose piece of concrete kerbing had punctured the right rear tyre. When practice resumed Jackie, undaunted from the incident, jumped into the MS80 initially set up for team mate Jean-Pierre Beltoise, but it was Jochen who took the £100 for that period.

In the final session try as he might Jackie could not squeeze that extra ounce of speed out of the Beltoise car and Jochen took pole position and the £100. I cannot recall a more exciting practice session at Silverstone. The scene was set for a very memorable grand prix.

During the race the duel continued through 62 of the 84 laps. At times Stewart and Rindt were swapping positions just feet apart. On lap 62 Rindt was forced to pit with an end plate on his rear aerofoil coming adrift and later on lap 77 he had to stop for fuel, this relegated him to fourth place with Jackie Stewart taking the flag for Ken Tyrell's Matra International team.

Jochen Rindt takes a relaxing stroll along the pit lane before his epic practice session duel with Jackie Stewart.

The determined Jackie Stewart sits patiently waiting for news of the Lotus team's lap times.

Jean-Pierre Beltoise

In 1969 Jackie Stewart was partnered in Ken Tyrell's Matra International équipe F1 team by a 32-year-old Frenchman Jean-Pierre Beltoise.

When the French driver Jean Behra was tragically killed in 1959, France lost its nationality on the F1 grids of the world championship. During the sixties however a number of new names had come to the fore, willing to race in the familiar blue colours of France.

Jean-Pierre Beltoise, a former motor cycle champion, was the one who seemed set for stardom when he changed from two wheels to four in 1963 and raced a 1.1 litre Rene Bonnet at Le Mans, winning the index of performance.

In 1964 however his motor racing career came to an abrupt halt following a terrifying accident at Rheims from which he received burns and multiple injuries.

This was not going to keep the determined Jean-Pierre from racing and in 1965 he was back racing in Formula 3 for Matra where he gave the new French team their first F3 win at Rheims, the circuit which nearly claimed his racing career.

Further successes encouraged Matra, the aerospace company, to pursue their motor racing interests even further and a Formula 2 team was established with Beltoise bringing home the European F2 championship title in 1968.

In 1969 Ken Tyrell and Matra confirmed Jean-Pierre as the number two driver to Jackie Stewart where he was a more than useful team driver.

At Silverstone for this race however, he could only manage ninth place with the four wheel drive MS84.

Jean-Pierre Beltoise later raced for BRM and pursued a successful career in sports and touring car races.

A smiling Jean-Pierre Beltoise in a crowded Silverstone pit lane.

Opposite: *In the cockpit of the Matra.*

127

Bruce McLaren

One of the most colourful teams in grand prix racing was of course the bright orange or tangerine McLarens to be driven by Bruce McLaren himself and team mate and fellow New Zealander Denny Hulme. Bruce McLaren was just 31 but had been in Formula 1 motor racing since 1959 when at the age of 22 he won the American Grand Prix at Sebring in a Cooper Climax and became the youngest ever driver to win a world championship race.

He won a New Zealand 'Driver to Europe Scholarship' in 1958 and began his career driving for Cooper in Formula 2 events. The twenty-year-old established quite a name for himself when he won the Formula 2 section of the German Grand Prix at the notorious Nurburgring circuit. Not only had he raced against the best cars and drivers in the world, but brought his F2 Cooper home in fifth place overall. This of course was at a time when Formula 1 and Formula 2 cars raced together in the championship.

Bruce continued with Cooper until 1965. The following year, he not only found time to win the Le Mans 24 Hour race in a Ford GT40 with another New Zealander, Chris Amon, but also set up his own racing team. Being both a talented driver and engineer Bruce designed and built his own car and the name McLaren has been in grand prix racing ever since. At first he suffered a number of problems, mostly associated with engines which were completely out of his control. By 1968 however the McLaren was using Ford Cosworth engines which launched them into a race winning team both in Formula 1 and sports car racing where they became CanAm Champions in 1967 and 1968.

In the 1969 British Grand Prix Bruce McLaren managed a third place in his Cosworth-powered V8 M7C after a duel with Jackie Ickx in his Brabham BT26.

In less than a year however, the sport lost the name of Bruce McLaren. On a sunny June afternoon at Goodwood, Bruce was testing his new CanAm M8D when a piece of bodywork flew from the car rendering it unstable. The car left the track and hit a marshal's post, Bruce died instantly.

Today the McLaren name lives on with today's world championship winning cars, a true testament to the friendly kiwi in the silver helmet and the tangerine car.

Opposite:
Bruce McLaren autographs a portrait of himself, presented by a photographer. This happened during a practice session in the Silverstone pits and is a testament to Bruce McLaren who was always one of the friendliest of grand prix drivers.

New Zealander Bruce McLaren in the Silverstone pits, one of the rare breed of designer, owner and racer. A brilliant engineer and successful driver whose name still lives on today with the highly successful McLaren Mercedes team.

Piers Courage

I was of course required to include a few shots of cars in action, but with only a photographer's pass available for one practice day I concentrated on pits and paddock activity. However, I did walk out to Copse Corner and experimented with action shots using slow shutter speeds and pans to promote movement. I was particularly pleased with my shot of Piers Courage in the Frank Williams' Brabham as it came towards me through Copse.

Piers had a particularly good race, starting in tenth place on the grid and after a race long duel with Graham Hill, eventually finished in fifth.

Piers Courage was a tremendously popular and charismatic figure, an ex-Etonian and destined for the family brewing business until he caught the racing bug. He learnt racing the hard way by towing his Formula 3 car around Europe on a trailer. He showed tremendous pace from an early stage and became a frequent winner. In 1965 he was presented with the Grovewood Award by Jim Clark as Britain's most promising young racing driver. He also married Lady Sarah 'Sally' Curzon with whom he had two sons.

His career progressed through Formula 3, Formula 2 and eventually into Formula 1 and drives with BRM. He also drove for his long standing friend Frank Williams in addition to trying his hand at endurance sports car racing.

Turning down an offer from Ferrari, he raced in Formula 1 for Frank Williams until tragedy struck in the 1970 Dutch Grand Prix at Zandvoort when he lost his life after his De Tomaso overturned and caught fire.

Piers Courage was just twenty-eight and described as one of the most promising drivers never to have realised his true potential.

Piers Courage rounds Copse Corner at speed in the Frank Williams Racing Brabham BT26 – Cosworth V8.

Piers Courage and his wife Sally at Thruxton in 1969.

Piers Courage at Brands Hatch with Reg Parnell's BRM in the 1968 British Grand Prix.

The Ferrari Drivers – Chris Amon and Pedro Rodriguez

Chris Amon has been described as one of the best drivers never to have won a championship grand prix. Despite a challenging career in which he raced both sports cars, Formula 2 and Formula 1, Chris Amon's career was always dogged by unreliability. It is said that fellow driver Mario Andretti once joked of Amon's race experiences saying "If he ever became an undertaker, people would stop dying".

However, after winning the 1966 Le Mans 24 Hour race in a 7 litre Ford GT40 Mk 11 with fellow New Zealander Bruce McLaren, he was summoned to Ferrari's headquarters at Maranello for a meeting with Enzo Ferrari himself. He subsequently signed to drive for Ferrari in Formula 1 and sports cars alongside Lorenzo Bandini, Ludovico Scarfiotti and Mike Parkes.

Chris Amon's career continued after leaving Ferrari in 1969 but he was continually dogged by bad luck. Following Niki Lauda's serious accident in the German Grand Prix of 1976, Amon announced his retirement from racing.

He did continue with a few drives in sports cars but gave up for good in 1978 returning to New Zealand and the family farm. His Formula 1 career had seen 102 grand prix races, 83 championship points and eleven podium finishes but never a grand prix win.

Silverstone in July 1969 was also one of his unlucky races despite being fourth on the grid; Chris Amon retired with a broken gearbox on Lap 45, whilst his team mate Pedro Rodriguez also suffered engine failure on Lap 61.

Pedro Rodriguez came from a wealthy Mexican family, who with his younger brother Ricardo raced motorcycles in their early teens. Racing some expensive and powerful cars funded by their father followed. This allowed the brothers to earn their reputations in racing even before their seventeenth birthdays.

Such was their potential that Ferrari importer to the US Luigi Chinetti arranged for Pedro at the age of 18 to drive a Ferrari 250 Testa Rossa at Le Mans with Jean Behra's son José. He returned fourteen times to Le Mans, eventually winning in 1968 with Lucien Bianchi in the famous John Wyer-Gulf Ford GT40.

Tragically, Pedro's younger brother Ricardo was killed in 1962 when practising for the Mexican Grand Prix. At this point Pedro considered retiring from racing. However he continued with drives in sports cars and Formula 1 until he himself was killed when in the lead, driving a Ferrari 512M sports car during the Interserie sports car race at the Norisring in Germany.

New Zealander Chris Amon prepares himself for a practice lap with the Ferrari V12.

Mexican Pedro Rodriguez left BRM to partner Chris Amon in the Ferrari V12.

John Miles

John Miles was the son of the actor Sir Bernard Miles. After studying engineering he started racing at club level in the mid sixties, taking third place in the Grovewood awards when driving for Willment in 1965.

In 1966 nine consecutive wins in a Willment-entered Lotus Elan brought his attention to the works Lotus team. During 1967 and 1968 he drove the GT Europas and Formula 3 cars with considerable success.

During 1969 Lotus entered him in Formula 2 events but after just three races, Colin Chapman entrusted the development of the four wheel drive Lotus 63 to Miles which he drove in five grand prix events.

Following Graham Hill's accident at Watkins Glen, Miles found himself team mate to Jochen Rindt for the 1970 season. He developed the Lotus 72 which Jochen raced so successfully until tragedy struck in the Italian Grand Prix at Monza.

Following Rindt's fatal accident and the recent deaths of Piers Courage and Bruce McLaren, John Miles retired from grand prix racing and began a life in technical journalism alongside his engineering career with Lotus.

The four wheel drive Lotus 63 Cosworth V8 is brought into Silverstone's marshalling area by a mechanic for John Miles' practice lap.

Opposite:
John Miles contemplates the development of the Lotus 63 prior to making a practice run.

Vic Elford – 'Quick Vic'

Not all F1 drivers were household names other than to the real motor racing enthusiast. One driver I always had a high regard for was Vic Elford who had a pedigree second to none. For the 1969 British Grand Prix Vic was entered in Colin Crabbe's Antique Automobiles McLaren Cosworth V8, establishing an eleventh place on the grid and bringing the car home in sixth place.

As an all round racing and rally driver few could match his range of experience and talent. He started racing a Mini in 1961 then rallying with a DKW in 1962. By 1967 he was driving for Porsche and later became synonymous with Porsche sports car racing and rallying eventually becoming European GT Rally Champion.

In 1968 he won the Monte Carlo Rally in a Porsche 911 and provided Porsche with their first ever outright win in the 24 Hours of Daytona in a 907. Successes in the Targa Florio, at the Nurburgring, Sebring, Monza and Laguna Seca, the list is endless, created the nickname 'Quick Vic'.

Perhaps his crowning glory was to be one of only two drivers ever to have achieved six major victories at the infamous Nurburgring, the other being Rudolf Caracciolo back in the 1920s.

Le Mans of course also features high in his driving record, having been the first driver ever to lap Le Mans at over 150mph. This was achieved in a Porsche 'long tail' 917 in 1970 which must have impressed Steve McQueen who hired him to drive some of the high speed action shots in the famous film *Le Mans*.

Vic retired from racing in the seventies and now lives in the USA.

I spotted this colour combination and motor racing still life in the Silverstone pits just after the practice sessions. Vic Elford's helmet and goggles hanging nonchalantly on the side of the car.

Opposite:
Vic Elford in the cockpit of the Antique Automobiles McLaren Ford.

Jo Siffert

Not coming from a wealthy background, Swiss-born Jo Siffert did everything possible to pay for his own racing and like a number of other racing drivers he came into the sport from racing motorcycles. His first event was in 1957 but went on to win the Swiss 350cc championship in 1959, eventually turning to four wheels with a Formula Junior Stanguellini in 1960.

'Seppi' as he was nicknamed managed wins in the 1961 season and finished joint European Formula Junior Champion before graduating to Formula 1 as a privateer in 1962 with a Lotus-Climax. He later drove for the Swiss team Scuderia Filipinetti.

One of Jo Siffert's most famous victories included the 1964 Mediterranean Grand Prix when he managed a win over none other than Jim Clark, repeating the same victory over Clark the following year.

Racing was always a financial struggle for Jo and his team who frequently slept in the open air to avoid the cost of hotel accommodation, a far cry from the luxurious surroundings and hospitality experienced by today's Formula 1 drivers.

It was British entrant Rob Walker, for whom Stirling Moss raced so successfully, who spotted the skill and determination of Jo Siffert. He was invited to drive for this famous name and continued to do so until the end of 1969.

During 1968 Rob Walker managed to obtain a Lotus 49B for Siffert to race in the British Grand Prix at Brands Hatch. However while undergoing repairs prior to the race, both Walker's garage and the car were destroyed by fire. Lotus came to the rescue with a replacement 49B which Siffert took to victory in a memorable race.

He went on to be victorious in sports cars, establishing many wins for the John Wyer Gulf Porsche Team. He also partnered Pedro Rodriguez in the BRM Formula 1 team with successes in Austria in 1971.

Jo Siffert was just 35 when in October 1971 tragedy struck at Brands Hatch during the Race of Champions. His car left the track and crashed heavily into the banking, the car bursting into flames, trapping him in the cockpit.

It was subsequently revealed that Jo Siffert had died of asphyxiation and the impact had only caused a broken leg. This accident led to a major review of motor racing safety both in car design and trackside fire facilities. Today, on board fire extinguishing systems and direct air injection into the driver's helmet are mandatory.

'Seppi' was regarded as a national hero in Switzerland. More than 50,000 people attended his funeral in Fribourg and a Porsche 917 in the John Wyer Gulf Team colours accompanied the hearse.

Jo Siffert and Graham Hill at Thruxton for a Formula 2 meeting in 1969.

Jo 'Seppi' Siffert photographed at Silverstone in July 1969 when he finished eighth in Rob Walker's Lotus 49B after a duel with Graham Hill and Piers Courage.

Ken Tyrell

Ken Tyrell was a Surrey timber merchant with a penchant for motor racing, which he tried with a Cooper back in the fifties, soon realising he was not driver material. It was not long before Ken was still immersed in the sport and running a team of cars from his woodshed at the family business. In the mid '60s he spotted a young Scot named Jackie Stewart and offered him a drive in his Formula 3 team. From that moment one of motor racing's most successful partnerships was established.

However, Jackie Stewart was a rising star and drove for BRM in F1 events until 1968 when Ken Tyrell was able to entice the young Scotsman back to the Tyrell fold with a Formula 1 drive.

With help from Ford and Elf the French petrol company, the Tyrell Formula 1 team was established with Ken Tyrell realising his ambition of seeing his own cars in Formula 1. He also became Team Principal for Matra International, a joint venture between Tyrell's own team and the French aerospace company and manufacturer, Matra.

In 1969 Jackie Stewart secured the world championship and again in 1971 and 1973. Tyrell also secured the constructors' title in 1971. This success story however was struck a mighty blow in 1973 at a time when Jackie Stewart had already secured the world championship at Monza. Stewart's close friend and team mate Francois Cevert was killed in practice following which Tyrell retired his team, handing the constructor's championship to Lotus.

Without their star driver and his French team mate, Tyrell were no longer a major force in Formula 1. Determined as ever Ken continued to race and with drivers Jody Scheckter, Patrick Depailler and Michele Alboreto still managed some grands prix victories.

The '80s and '90s saw mixed fortune for Tyrell. In 1998 struggling with both success and ill health Ken, at the age of 73 sold his team to British American Tobacco. The Tyrell name disappeared and the team became British American Racing.

Ken Tyrell or 'Uncle Ken' as he was affectionately known died of cancer in August 2001. During his career he had introduced more talented racing drivers into the sport than anyone. His team had recorded 33 Formula 1 race victories and above all he had become one of the most respected and admired ambassadors of the sport.

Opposite: *Ken Tyrell (Uncle Ken)*.

Carrying the No 1 for world championship status, Jackie Stewart passes the Silverstone pits in the famous blue Matra colours of the Tyrell team. (Photographed in 1971).

Jackie Stewart – World Champion 1969.

The Last Lap

In this book I can only hope that I have achieved the brief laid down by Agfa Gevaert in providing me with such an opportunity and that my now historical photographs continue to provide lasting enjoyment to the reader.

The sport has given me immense satisfaction over the years and I am extremely proud to have witnessed and photographed some of motor racing's classic moments.

In this book I have tried to identify the scene as accurately as possible and much of the racing data has been taken from the programmes, reports and press handouts which I have kept over the years. I trust therefore that I have not offended anyone who may appear in some of my images and who is unnamed, but memory takes its toll over the years and any omission or error is entirely unintentional.

1969 was my final year working for Agfa Gevaert and a world championship year for Jackie Stewart and Ken Tyrell. I will be eternally grateful to have photographed just a small part of their magnificent achievement.

Finally, I would like to take this opportunity to pay tribute to those drivers who allowed me to intrude into their sometimes private world during times which could be quietly intense or full of excitement and celebration.

Motor racing has been described as a cruel sport and indeed it can be, particularly the era covered by this book. Many of the drivers featured are no longer with us and those that remain have done much to improve circuit safety and race car design.

Although still a sport of speed and danger, there is no doubt that motor racing today has become a much safer environment. Much credit for this must go to Sir Jackie Stewart OBE who has pioneered and achieved significant safety standards within the sport.

Roger Lane. July 2009